STECK-VAUGHN
PORTRAIT OF AMERICA

Connecticut

Steck-Vaughn Company

Executive Editor	Diane Sharpe
Senior Editor	Martin S. Saiewitz
Design Manager	Pamela Heaney
Photo Editor	Margie Foster

Proof Positive/Farrowlyne Associates, Inc.
Program Editorial, Revision Development, Design, and Production

Consultant: Bruce Fraser, Executive Director, Connecticut Humanities Council

Published by Raintree Steck-Vaughn Publishers, an imprint of Steck-Vaughn Company.

A Turner Educational Services, Inc. book. Based on the Portrait of America television series by R. E. (Ted) Turner.

Cover Photo: Mystic Seaport by © Comstock.

Library of Congress Cataloging-in-Publication Data

Thompson, Kathleen.
    Connecticut / Kathleen Thompson.
       p.   cm. — (Portrait of America)
    "Based on the Portrait of America television series"—T.p. verso.
    "A Turner book."
    Includes index.
    ISBN 0-8114-7327-9 (library binding).—ISBN 0-8114-7432-1 (softcover)
    1. Connecticut—Juvenile literature. [1. Connecticut.]
  I. Title. II. Series: Thompson, Kathleen. Portrait of America.
  F94.3.T46 1996
  974—dc20   95-22843
                                        CIP
                                        AC

Printed and Bound in the United States of America

1 2 3 4 5 6 7 8 9 10 WZ 98 97 96 95

Acknowledgments
The publishers wish to thank the following for permission to reproduce photographs:
Pp. 7, 8, 10 Connecticut Department of Economic Development; p. 11 Courtesy The First Church in Windsor, United Church of Christ; p. 12 North Wind Picture Archives; p. 13 US Navy; p. 14 Reagan Bradshaw; p. 15 The Bettmann Archive; p. 17 Courtesy Goodyear Tire Company; p. 18 Connecticut Department of Economic Development; p. 21 Courtesy Merriam-Webster Inc.; p. 22 Painted by Edwin B. Child in 1933, Merriam-Webster Inc.; p. 23 Reagan Bradshaw, used with permission of Merriam-Webster Inc.; p. 24 © Nathan Benn/Stock Boston; p. 26 Connecticut Department of Economic Development; pp. 28 & 29 © Wayne Eastep; pp. 30 & 31 Courtesy Kaman Corporation; p. 32 © Michael Marsland/Yale University; p. 34 Sophia Smith Collection; p. 35 (top) The Mark Twain House, Hartford, CT, (bottom) The Connecticut Historical Society; p. 36 Connecticut Department of Economic Development; p. 37 W. B. Carter/Yale University; pp. 38 & 39 Connecticut Junior Republic; pp. 40 & 41 Connecticut's Mystic & More CVB; pp. 42 & 44 © Superstock; p. 46 One Mile Up; p. 47 (left) One Mile Up, (center) © Thomas Hovland/Grant Heilman Photography, (right) © Vireo.

STECK-VAUGHN
PORTRAIT OF AMERICA

Connecticut

Kathleen Thompson

A Turner Book

RSVP

RAINTREE
STECK-VAUGHN
PUBLISHERS
The Steck-Vaughn Company

Austin, Texas

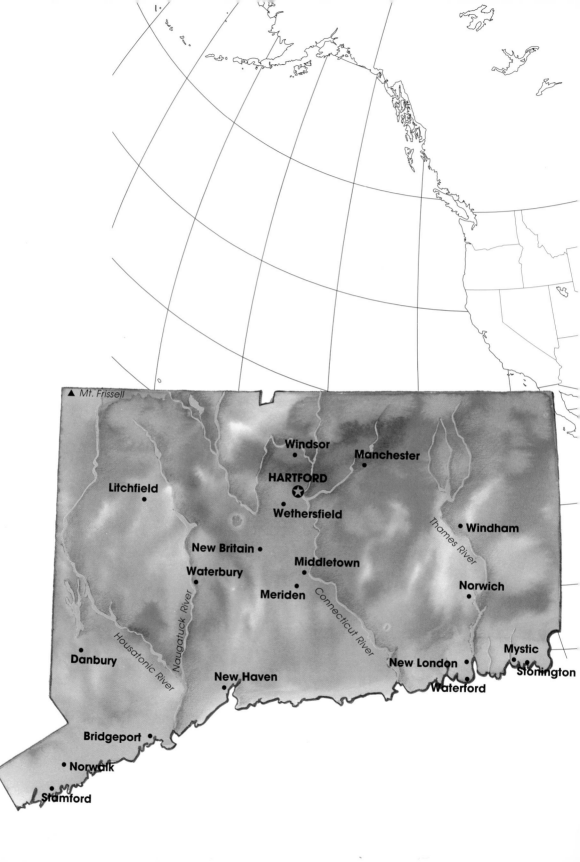

Connecticut

▲ Mt. Frissell

Windsor

Manchester

HARTFORD ★

Litchfield

Wethersfield

Windham

Thames River

New Britain

Middletown

Waterbury

Meriden

Norwich

Connecticut River

Naugatuck River

Housatonic River

Danbury

Mystic

New London

New Haven

Stonington

Waterford

Bridgeport

Norwalk

Stamford

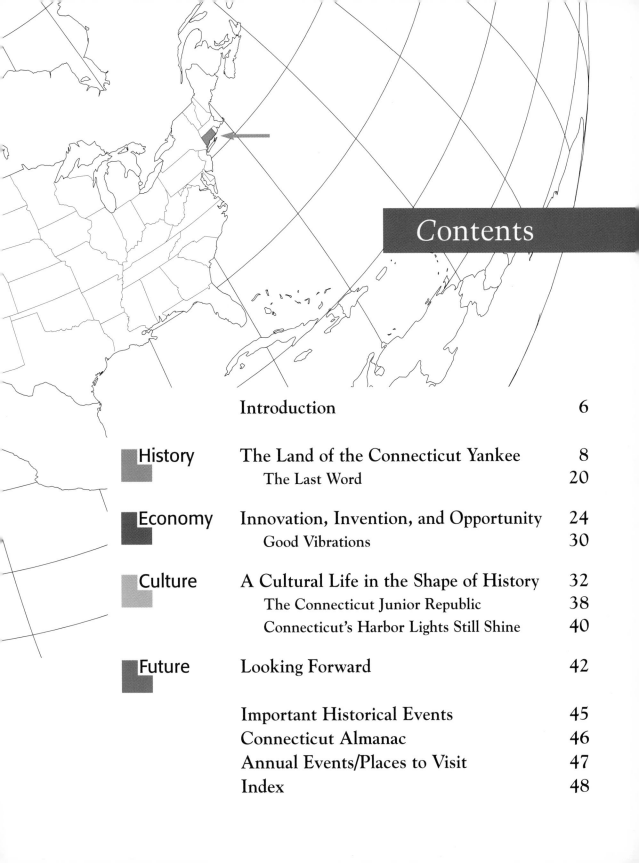

Contents

Introduction   6

History   The Land of the Connecticut Yankee   8
               The Last Word   20

Economy   Innovation, Invention, and Opportunity   24
               Good Vibrations   30

Culture   A Cultural Life in the Shape of History   32
               The Connecticut Junior Republic   38
               Connecticut's Harbor Lights Still Shine   40

Future   Looking Forward   42

           Important Historical Events   45
           Connecticut Almanac   46
           Annual Events/Places to Visit   47
           Index   48

Introduction

Connecticut is richer in natural beauty than in natural resources. Neither forests, minerals, nor stony soil offer the people prosperity. So they have always relied on their heads and their hands to make their living. And they have succeeded. Few states have produced so many good ideas—or put them to better use. Connecticut's colonial system of laws became a model for the United States Constitution. The suggestion that the new nation's congress should have two houses came from a Connecticut delegate. The idea of manufacturing products from other states' raw materials solved a problem, too. It has been the source of Connecticut's prosperity from the days of wooden ships to the days of nuclear submarines.

Mystic Seaport, a re-creation of a nineteenth-century whaling village, brings more tourists to Connecticut than any other attraction in the state.

Connecticut

anufacturing, insurance, clocks, inventors

The Land of the Connecticut Yankee

Twelve thousand years ago, Native Americans lived on the land we call Connecticut. Archaeologists have discovered many things about them by digging for, finding, and studying the traces of the civilization that they left behind. We know they hunted with arrows, spears, and knives. Recently archaeologists found an arrowhead too small to kill anything. It may have belonged to a child.

When the first Europeans came to Connecticut, they met the descendants of these prehistoric Native Americans. We call these descendants the Algonquins. The Pequot were the most powerful of the Algonquins. The Pequot lived in southern Connecticut, near the Thames River. For a time the Pequot lived with another large group called the Mohegan. There were also other groups in the area. When the Dutch explorer Adriaen Block sailed up the Connecticut River in 1614, almost seven thousand Native Americans lived in the region.

The gold-domed State Capitol in Hartford was designed in 1879 and resembles a Gothic cathedral.

Adriaen Block was the first European to come into Connecticut; he claimed the land for his country, Holland. All Europeans did this in the early days of exploration. Nineteen years later, the Dutch built a small fort called "House of Hope" at the place where Hartford now stands. But they didn't settle there permanently.

The first permanent settlers were English. Most of them didn't come directly from England. Instead, in 1633, they moved to Connecticut from the Massachusetts Bay Colony. Their leader was a man named Thomas Hooker. He and his group founded Hartford, located in the middle of the Connecticut region. Two more villages—Wethersfield and Windsor—were settled around this time. Together, the three villages formed the Connecticut Colony.

The Connecticut settlers had trouble with their neighbors. The settlers feared the Pequot, who controlled half of Connecticut. The Pequot felt threatened by the settlers, who were taking over Native American land. Then, in 1636 a Pequot was accused of murdering a colonist. The Mohegan and the Narragansett groups joined with the settlers and attacked a Pequot village and fort. They burned the village down and in that one attack killed about six hundred Pequot men, women, and children. Within a few weeks the colonists captured most of the remaining Pequot and sold them into slavery. Only a few Pequot have survived in America.

This cloth bag and other Native American artifacts on display in Connecticut's museums provide insight into the traditional culture of Native Americans.

In 1639 the Connecticut Colony adopted a set of laws called the Fundamental Orders. These laws were based on one of Thomas Hooker's deepest beliefs: Government should be based on the consent of the people being governed. This familiar idea is still important to all of us today. Why? Because one of the models for the Constitution of the United States came from this very same idea.

The first church in Windsor was built in 1794. The church was first organized in 1630.

In the early days there was freedom of worship in Connecticut—if you were a Congregationalist. Like many American colonists, the people of Connecticut had come from England in search of religious freedom for their own religion, not for all religions. Freedom for all religions would not come for a long time. In fact, the Congregational Church was the established church in Connecticut until 1818.

As the years went by, more towns joined the Connecticut Colony. Other towns joined the New Haven Colony, which was located on the east coast of the region. Then, in 1662 England gave the Connecticut Colony a royal charter. Unlike some of the other royal colonies, Connecticut was given self-rule. The boundaries set by the charter included all of the New Haven Colony. New Haven didn't like that fact very much. Finally, after three years of arguing, the two colonies united in 1665. But things weren't completely settled. For two hundred years, the capital of Connecticut alternated between New Haven and Hartford.

Not everyone liked the idea that Connecticut was so independent. When Sir Edmund Andros became the royal governor of several other New England colonies, he wanted to control Connecticut, too. In 1687 he went to Hartford himself and demanded that the people give their charter to him.

The story of the Charter Oak may be part legend.

What happened next is probably part truth and part fable. According to the story, one evening the colonists had a candle-lit meeting with Andros. When the colonists realized Andros was trying to take their charter, suddenly all the candles in the meeting room went out. When they were relit, the charter was gone. In the darkness, someone had whisked the document out of the room and hidden it in a hollow oak tree. Since that night, people have referred to this tree as the Charter Oak.

Connecticut was a small colony, proud of its independence. But it soon became clear that the colony didn't have enough land. Farming couldn't support everyone. People had to find something else to do. So, Connecticut became one of the earliest manufacturing regions. People started making things to sell.

Connecticut workers made ships and clocks. They worked in silver and tin. They started selling their products all over New England. Their salesmen became known as "Yankee peddlers."

The Yankee peddlers were successful. So was manufacturing in Connecticut. When the Revolutionary War began, the state's ability to manufacture war materials became very important to the rest of the colonies. From 1775 until the end of the war, Connecticut provided food, cloth for uniforms, and weapons. That tradition continues up to the present day. Some people have called Connecticut "the arsenal of democracy" because it has made so many of the weapons used in wars the United States has fought. Connecticut also supplied many soldiers to Washington's army.

On June 14, 1776, Connecticut's Assembly passed a resolution in favor of independence from Great Britain. Connecticut was also one of the 13 colonies that later signed the Declaration of Independence. During the course of the Revolutionary War, the British attacked Connecticut's coastline towns.

After the war, the states gathered to discuss their future at the Constitutional Convention in 1787. The states became locked in a debate about the best way to

U.S. Government photo

The *Turtle* was an early submarine that was designed by a Yale student and built in Connecticut. It was hand-driven, and it was used briefly in the Revolutionary War.

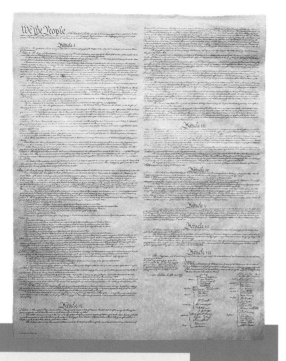

One of the models for the United States Constitution was Connecticut's Fundamental Orders. The Orders, adopted in 1639, are thought to be the first example of a written democratic constitution.

represent each state in Congress. Larger states wanted to base the number of representatives on each state's population. The smaller states wanted each state to have an equal number of votes.

Finally, a Connecticut man, Roger Sherman, came up with a suggestion. Why not have two houses of Congress? In one, the House of Representatives, representation would be based on how many people lived in a state. In the other, the Senate, each state would have an equal number of representatives—two. Sherman's solution, which was called the Connecticut Compromise, solved the problem. Connecticut was the fifth state to join the Union.

In the second half of the eighteenth century, Connecticut ran into economic hard times. Although parts of the state were solely concerned with manufacturing, farming was still the main occupation. Over time, families grew, and more and more immigrants arrived. In the early 1800s it became clear that Connecticut was too small. There weren't enough farms to meet the needs of the growing population. People throughout the state complained about the lack of space. Connecticut people moved out of the state by the thousands. Many of them were farmers looking for more or better land. Others who left went on to make their name elsewhere. The state lost good people, but the rest of the country was benefiting.

For instance, in 1831, almost one third of the members of the United States Senate had been born in Connecticut. And almost one quarter of the House of Representatives was made up of individuals from this small state. The Austin family left Connecticut and founded an early settlement in Texas. The Huntingtons went to California and built railroads and museums. The Newberrys became one of the most powerful families in Chicago.

Meanwhile, Connecticut increasingly manufactured goods for sale to other states. By the end of the eighteenth century, the fertile imaginations of Connecticut inventors gave manufacturing a tremendous boost. Many devices they invented at this time made manufacturing of certain goods quicker and easier.

The United States Patent Office issued 1,179 patents, or licenses, between 1790 and 1810. One of the most important of these was the cotton gin in 1793. Eli Whitney's invention had a tremendous impact on cotton production in the South.

Later, Eli Whitney moved to Connecticut and went to work for a gun-making company. There he came up with an idea that changed the manufacturing industry: If all the guns of a certain kind had parts that were exactly alike, they would all be easier to assemble and repair. Spare parts could be made before the gun needed to be repaired. Eli Whitney's simple idea marked the beginning of mass production. Before Whitney came up with his idea, a gunsmith (or a maker of anything, from pots and pans to snowshoes) made one item at a time, part by part. Today, very few things are made in that

Roger Sherman was the Connecticut citizen who thought of the idea of having two houses in the United States Congress.

way. Whitney's new way of manufacturing was the beginning of modern technology.

Eli Terry used Whitney's idea to mass-produce clocks. Rodney and Horatio Hanks opened a silk mill, the first in the country. And Connecticut inventors kept on inventing. A man named David Bushnell invented a workable submarine. Charles Goodyear came up with a way to strengthen rubber. A woman named Mrs. Prout made the first American cigar. Since those early days, Connecticut inventors have been responsible for everything from the coffee mill to the corkscrew to the portable typewriter.

By the 1840s, people were moving to Connecticut instead of away. The state built roads and railways to bring raw materials in and take finished goods out. More factories were built to make buttons, hats, coins, and nuts and bolts. By the 1850s, more people in Connecticut worked in manufacturing than in agriculture. During the Civil War, the state's factories turned out guns, ammunition, and other goods that the Union Army needed to fight the Confederacy.

After the war, immigration became a major fact of life in the United States. Thousands of people moved to the United States from Europe. A lot of these people went to work in Connecticut's factories. Even people born and raised on Connecticut farms went to work in the state's industries. By 1910 almost ninety percent of the state's people lived in cities. By that same year, almost one third of the people in the state had been born outside of America.

This painting features Charles Goodyear, who, in 1839, discovered a way to make rubber stronger.

During both World War I and World War II, Connecticut was again a major supplier of war materials. Later, in 1954, Connecticut shipbuilders introduced the first nuclear-powered submarine, the *Nautilus*.

By the 1960s the United States was looking to expand transportation to another level. The country was in a "space race" with Russia. Connecticut manufacturers built reentry vehicles for spacecraft. When the first person stepped onto the moon, he carried his oxygen and other supplies in a backpack made in Connecticut.

In 1964 a major change came to Connecticut politics. For over three hundred years, Connecticut had three levels of government: state government, county government, and towns. The state had more than 160 townships altogether. Each town had a strong local government. Each of those towns, no matter how big or how small, could elect the same number of representatives to the state legislature. However, this system meant that only about ten percent of the people could elect a majority in the legislature.

In 1964 a federal court ruled that this law was not constitutional. In 1965 the state created a new set of legislative districts. This new policy shifted much of the political power from small towns to large cities.

The U.S. Naval Submarine Base in Groton was the site of the construction and launching of the world's first nuclear-powered submarine, the *Nautilus,* in 1954. The site is now a memorial and visitors can board the historic vessel.

There was one other significant change during the 1960s. Many large United States cities experienced riots. Connecticut cities were hit, too. There was rioting in the streets of Hartford. Connecticut cities, alarmed by the violence, responded to the challenge. Hartford corporations began to cooperate with community groups to offer job-training programs. Decent housing was constructed in some poor economic areas. Hartford elected an African American mayor, and other minority politicians began to help Connecticut's cities deal with the poverty that existed side by side with the state's great wealth.

In the 1980s and 1990s, Connecticut had another common problem in its urban areas. Many of the state's wealthier citizens moved out of the cities in greater numbers. As a result, cities found it harder to pay for schools and other city services. Finally, in 1991, Governor Lowell Weicker, Jr., imposed a state income tax, something the state had never had in its history. Some of the money generated from this tax went toward helping troubled urban areas. The state also legalized gambling, which brought in more money. In fact, the descendants of the Pequot opened a gambling casino on their reservation. It is the only casino on the East Coast outside of the ones in Atlantic City, New Jersey.

The challenges that face Connecticut will continue. But one thing is certain: Connecticut Yankees will continue to solve their problems with creativity, flexibility, and determination.

The Last Word

What do you do when you want to learn the meaning of a certain word? If you're like most people, you do one of two things. You ask someone to tell you the word's meaning, or you look up the word in a dictionary.

The fact that you can look up words in a dictionary can be traced to a man named Noah Webster. He produced the first dictionary of American English.

Noah Webster was a person who loved words. He was born in West Hartford, Connecticut, in 1758. Webster studied at Yale and later became a teacher and a writer.

In 1782 Webster was teaching at an elementary school in Goshen, New York. He saw that the schoolbooks he was using had left out something he felt was important. The books Webster had to use in his teaching came from England. These books were just fine for teaching English children. But they paid no attention to American culture. Remember, the United States had only just won its independence from England. Americans still educated their children the same way the British did. Noah Webster wanted to give his students an education that was strongly American.

To do this, in 1783 he published a spelling book for schoolchildren. Its full title was *The American Spelling Book*, but it came to be known as the "Blue-Backed Speller." The spelling guide became very popular. Over the years, it sold more than a hundred million copies. Copies were still being sold during much of the 1900s.

The spelling book gave Webster the idea for a dictionary of American word usage. Webster published his first dictionary in 1806. It was called the *Compendious Dictionary of the English Language*. (Look up *compendious* in a Webster's dictionary!) Webster wanted this book to help set rules of American spelling. It contained only about a thousand words.

This dictionary was important because Webster included ideas that dictionaries never had before. One of these ideas was to give the letters *i* and *j* their own sections. Before Webster, writers of dictionaries had always included those letters under one heading. Webster also made many spellings simpler and different from those in Britain. He saw no reason for the extra letters in many British spellings. For example, at that time the British spelled the final consonant sound of the word *music* with a *ck*—*musick*. In Webster's first dictionary he dropped the *k* and left it simply *music*. His spelling is the one we use today.

In writing his first dictionary, Webster was preparing for something grander. He had become familiar with many different languages. He felt it was helpful and important to know where words came from—their histories. He traveled in England and France doing research on the histories of English words.

AN

AMERICAN DICTIONARY

OF THE

ENGLISH LANGUAGE:

INTENDED TO EXHIBIT,

I. The origin, affinities and primary signification of English words, as far as they have been ascertained.
II. The genuine orthography and pronunciation of words, according to general usage, or to just principles of analogy.
III. Accurate and discriminating definitions, with numerous authorities and illustrations.

TO WHICH ARE PREFIXED,

AN INTRODUCTORY DISSERTATION

ON THE

ORIGIN, HISTORY AND CONNECTION OF THE

LANGUAGES OF WESTERN ASIA AND OF EUROPE,

AND A CONCISE GRAMMAR

OF THE

ENGLISH LANGUAGE.

BY NOAH WEBSTER, LL. D.

IN TWO VOLUMES.

VOL. I.

He that wishes to be counted among the benefactors of posterity, must add, by his own toil, to the acquisitions of his ancestors.—*Rambler.*

NEW YORK:
PUBLISHED BY S. CONVERSE.
PRINTED BY HEZEKIAH HOWE—NEW HAVEN.
1828.

The title page of the first edition of Noah Webster's dictionary announces his grand intention of providing a completely thorough guide to the spelling, historical origins, pronunciation, and usage of English-language words.

Noah Webster believed that grammar and spelling should be taught to reflect the language as it is commonly spoken.

a quill pen, which was a feather with its thickest end sharpened into a point. This point was dipped in a bottle of ink in order to write. A writer using a quill pen had to dip the pen constantly to refill the ink.

Webster's *An American Dictionary of the English Language* was published in two volumes and had seventy thousand entries. About thirty thousand of these definitions had never before appeared in a dictionary. Many people did not like this new dictionary. They said that Webster used too many American spellings and not enough of the British ones they were used to. They called the new spellings "Americanisms."

The new dictionary sold well in the first year. But the negative public opinion influenced sales. The dictionary did not sell well after that. Webster published an updated version of the dictionary in 1841. This one was completely unsuccessful.

After Noah Webster died in 1843, George and Charles Merriam bought the rights to his dictionary.

In 1807 he began work on *An American Dictionary of the English Language*. Webster was seventy years old when he published the first edition of this important work in 1828.

Webster wrote the dictionary completely by hand. In those days people didn't have ballpoint pens, much less typewriters. He had to use

They formed a company called Merriam-Webster to publish it. The Merriam-Webster company continues to produce dictionaries. They are some of the most popular dictionaries in the world.

Part of the impact of Webster's work was to show that an American culture had begun to form in this country. It was an important step in gaining total independence from England.

Our language—which we still call English—continues to grow and change, as languages do. As a result, dictionaries have to be updated. Noah Webster understood this more than two hundred years ago. You might even say that this man who loved words still gets the last word.

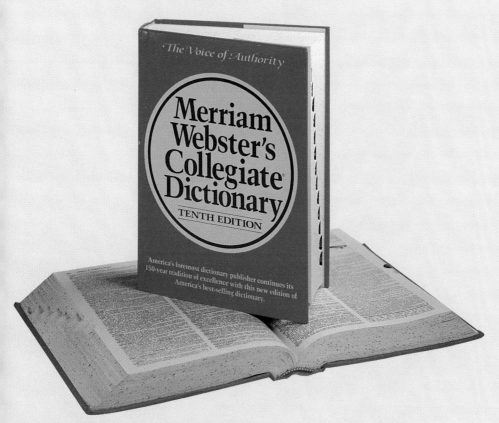

In 1993 Merriam-Webster published the tenth edition of its collegiate dictionary, with many new words added.

Innovation, Invention, and Opportunity

At first glance, Connecticut doesn't seem to have much going for it economically. It's a small state, without much open land. What open land exists is not good farmland. The soil is rocky, but the rocks don't conceal rich minerals. All Connecticut really has is beauty and people. But they're enough.

Because its people are so resourceful, Connecticut became a major industrial state. Industries that provide services are the biggest part of its economy. But manufacturing provides about twenty percent of the state's annual income. Most of the raw materials used in manufacturing come from somewhere else.

Connecticut's manufacturing history began way back in the 1600s. By the early 1800s, there were mass production and interchangeable parts. Over the years Connecticut's industry has proven it can adapt.

For example, Connecticut once produced almost all the hats that were made in this country. Then people stopped wearing hats, so the manufacturers went on to make something else. In colonial times,

Thousands of people choose to live in Connecticut and commute to their jobs in New York City.

the Connecticut Leather Company—Coleco—made leather goods for shoemakers. Later the company got into another line of work. It became a national leader in electronic games.

Connecticut has always had many different industries. That variety has made the economy stable and has usually kept the unemployment figures very low. About 25 percent of Connecticut's population is directly employed in manufacturing. The largest area of manufacturing is transportation equipment. But in

Connecticut is a leading manufacturer of aircraft and also has the largest flight museum in the Northeast. The New England Air Museum in Windsor Locks exhibits a wide variety of aircraft dating from 1909 to the present.

this state they don't make automobiles. What they do make is aircraft. The state is a leader in the production of helicopters and jet aircraft engines. Connecticut factories also make submarines and small boats.

The manufacturing area that comes in second is nonelectric machinery. That category covers a lot. But one large part of this kind of manufacturing is making machines that make other things. Connecticut factories don't make shoes, but they make machines to make shoes. Connecticut is one of the largest machine-tool manufacturing states in the country.

Fabricated metal products are the next most important manufacturing area. Fabricated metals include everything from knives and forks to nuts and bolts. Connecticut factories make corkscrews, can openers, and pipe fittings. And many things they make were also invented here in the state.

Other important types of manufacturing include electric machinery and scientific equipment. That means everything from laser technology to lamps and electric mixers. The list of things that are made in Connecticut goes on and on. Some other items, such as clocks and silverware, have been manufactured here for over three hundred years. Some, such as chemical products, are part of modern technology.

Hartford is sometimes referred to as the insurance capital of the world. Certainly, many large insurance companies have made their headquarters in the state. In a way, the story of insurance in Hartford began in Chicago. After the Chicago fire in 1871, insurance claims from burned homes and businesses flooded insurance companies. There were so many expensive claims that many insurance companies went bankrupt. Seeing an opportunity, the president of the Phoenix Insurance Company in Hartford, Connecticut, got on a train and went to Chicago. He stood on a soapbox on the shore of Lake Michigan and declared, "Phoenix of Hartford will pay all claims." From that time on, Hartford's reputation was made.

Today, insurance—including real estate and finance—employs almost ten percent of Connecticut's population. That may not seem too large until you realize that farming employs only a little over one percent. Agriculture also accounts for about one percent of the value of goods produced in the state. The largest part of that comes from greenhouse and nursery products. Eggs and milk are another important part of Connecticut's total farm output.

The biggest crop in Connecticut is shade tobacco. These plants are grown under a tentlike structure to keep the sun off them. As a result, the plants produce a very fine tobacco leaf that is used to wrap cigars. Once, this farm product was even more important to the state. Then someone invented a way to make cigar wrappers out of regular tobacco, using a process that was like the one for making paper. That meant shade tobacco was no longer so necessary to the cigar industry. (The man who invented the new wrapper was, of course, from Connecticut.) Many farmers shifted to other crops, but tobacco still remains Connecticut's largest field crop.

Shade tobacco is used as the outer wrapper in cigars.

This gauze netting is used to protect shade tobacco from direct sunlight.

An increasingly important industry in the state is tourism. Connecticut is in New England, but the weather doesn't get as cold as it does in Maine or Vermont. It's just over the border from New York. And it's a lovely place.

So, many people from New York and other nearby states come into Connecticut. They enjoy the ocean beaches, the old country inns, and the many rivers and lakes. Others come to ski in winter or visit the beautiful small towns and the state's historical museums. Many people own summer homes in Connecticut. The rich and famous find it a place where people will leave them alone.

So it's true that all Connecticut really has are beauty and people. But now, as it was three hundred years ago, that's enough.

Good Vibrations

It was the 1940s, and Charlie Kaman's business began like many businesses. He had an idea about how to make a better product. And what a product! Charlie Kaman set off on his own to make helicopters. At the time, he was just an inventor with an idea. But a lot of things in Connecticut have started with just an inventor and an idea. Although Mr. Kaman didn't really have enough money to start a business, he didn't let that stop him. "The Kaman Corporation started in 1945 with two thousand dollars" Mr. Kaman said. "And that's the great American story, that we could do that and survive and grow. . . ."

The idea was to build a helicopter that anyone could fly . . . "to the drug-store for a tube of toothpaste." Most of us don't fly our helicopters to the drugstore. But the Kaman Corporation

certainly succeeded in making many of the world's best helicopters.

The company makes other things as well. One of them was another great idea of Charlie Kaman. It's a good example of how the mind of an inventor has to work to become successful. Mr. Kaman took what he learned working on helicopters and invented the round-backed guitar.

Mr. Kaman explains how he made the unlikely leap from helicopters to guitars. "Well, for years, the whole problem in helicopters was to make them not shake. . . . You've got this

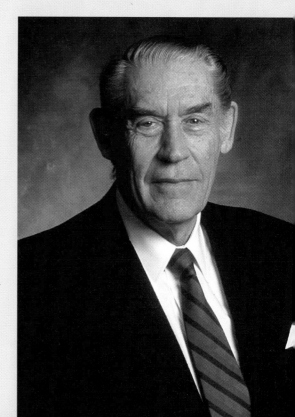

Charles H. Kaman is the founder, chairman, and chief executive officer of Kaman Corporation. His Connecticut-based company employs some five thousand people in the United States, Canada, and Europe.

Kaman Corporation is a leader in the music industry, manufacturing the Ovation and Hamer guitars as well as amplifiers and sound systems.

Kaman Corporation has developed K-MAX, the world's first commercial helicopter specifically designed for vertical lift.

rotor turning up here, with all kinds of harmonics coming down. Aerodynamics, dynamics, excitation—that makes them shake." Mr. Kaman had studied vibrations for years, so he understood them. He knew he could make a good guitar. Why? He let us in on the secret. "This guitar—to make it good, it *must* shake, so you do the opposite."

The Kaman Corporation did exactly the opposite and created the Ovation guitar. Mr. Kaman and the Kaman Corporation are prime examples of Yankee ingenuity. Something else is involved, too. As Charlie Kaman said, "Yes, it is small potatoes compared to the rest of our business. But it's fun potatoes."

A Cultural Life in the Shape of History

Much of the culture of Connecticut is rooted in its past. Many of its fine libraries began long ago. So did some of its universities. Yale University and its library were founded in 1701. Both are still flourishing. Eli Whitney's original cotton gin is displayed in one of Connecticut's museums. A major Connecticut newspaper, *The Hartford Courant*, has been publishing longer than any other newspaper in the United States. It began in 1764.

The most visible part of Connecticut's culture is rooted firmly in its history. Connecticut is known for its fine colonial architecture and picturesque town squares. In colonial times important public buildings were built around the central public park, called a green. Many colonial towns have worked to restore these fine buildings. All over the state, people have restored old homes—even whole villages—so all of us can see what they were like when the United States began.

Yale University in New Haven is one of the oldest and most respected universities in the United States.

One place is very special to Connecticut. In the nineteenth century many of America's whaling ships sailed out of the state's seaports. Today, visitors to Mystic Seaport step back into those days. This town on Mystic Harbor has been called a "living museum." This is because there is so much authentic maritime history still available to see and touch.

Education and schools were very important to early Connecticut citizens. The first school began in 1637. A famous school for the deaf was founded by Thomas H. Gallaudet in 1817. It still exists in West Hartford. Prudence Crandall opened a school for African American girls in 1833. And, of course, Noah Webster wrote his dictionary and his textbooks for young children in the early 1800s.

Because early colonists believed education was important, education gave rise to much of the literature written in Connecticut's early years. Jonathan Edwards was a Puritan minister. He wrote sermons designed to teach his strict view of God and the universe. Another educator, Amos Bronson Alcott, wrote verses and essays about his ideas for a perfect human community.

Harriet Beecher Stowe, who lived much of her life in Connecticut, wrote the novel *Uncle Tom's Cabin*. The book was intended to awaken the country to the horrors of slavery. And she succeeded. When Abraham Lincoln met her for the first time, he is reported to have remarked, "So, you're the lady who started the Civil War." Mark Twain was born in Missouri, but he moved to Connecticut. While he lived there he wrote

The publication of *Uncle Tom's Cabin* in 1853 brought Harriet Beecher Stowe immediate fame.

Mark Twain wrote some of his best works during the twenty years he lived in Hartford, Connecticut, including *The Adventures of Tom Sawyer* and *The Adventures of Huckleberry Finn.*

William Gillette portrayed Sherlock Holmes on stage as well as in a 1915 movie.

A Connecticut Yankee in King Arthur's Court. Sloan Wilson, a native Connecticut writer, penned *The Man in the Grey Flannel Suit.* This novel showed the difficulty of life in the business world.

But not all of Connecticut's artists have been so serious. Actor William Gillette made his name and his fortune playing the detective Sherlock Holmes. On his Connecticut estate, he built his own railroad and took his guests for rides around the lawn. He also built a castle and a houseboat and rode a motorcycle.

Another Connecticut actor, James O'Neill, became famous for playing the title role in *The Count*

William Gillette built the 24-room Gillette Castle between 1914 and 1919.

of Monte Cristo. He was even more famous for being the father of a playwright. His son Eugene O'Neill is considered by many people to be the greatest playwright this country has ever produced.

Today, culture still thrives in Connecticut. The state can boast of four symphony orchestras. Yale University has the oldest and one of the country's best university art museums. In addition, the Wadsworth Atheneum is another of the oldest public art museums. At the Atheneum, Americans first saw the work of Pablo Picasso, who many consider to be among the world's finest painters.

Connecticut's contribution to theater includes the Yale School of Drama, which is famous for such graduates as Meryl Streep. The National Theatre of the Deaf has built a fine reputation in Connecticut. So has the Goodspeed Opera House, which helps to develop new musical theater. Perhaps the most important theater is the Eugene O'Neill Theater Center in Waterford. The center includes the National Institute for Theater, which instructs young actors, and the National Critics Conference, which trains theater critics. It also includes the Eugene O'Neill National Playwrights' Conference. The conference provides a place where playwrights can work on their new plays.

Connecticut is home to groups from many other cultures, too. Among them are the Portuguese fishing community in Stonington, the Italian neighborhoods of New Haven, and the Polish areas of New Britain. All of them have contributed to the art, music, literature, and quality of life in Connecticut.

The Yale Repertory Theatre is a place where professional actors learn their art.

The Connecticut Junior Republic

"Stealing and school. I stole and I didn't go to school—never home, doing things wrong, getting caught for them. And they finally caught up with me. That's why I'm here."

These are the words of Kevin Holmgren, an unusual Connecticut resident. He said them when he was living in northwestern Connecticut, in a town called Litchfield. It's a beautiful town with a lot of New England charm. The houses are old and graceful. Many of its people are very wealthy.

But Litchfield's people also believe in duty. And part of what they see as their duty is helping people who have not had their good fortune. Mary Buel showed her sense of duty when she decided to give her farm, plus a great deal of money, to help people less fortunate then she was. That farm became the Connecticut Junior Republic.

Residents participate in activities at the Connecticut Junior Republic.

The two hundred acres of land that are part of the Connecticut Junior Republic's residential campus in Litchfield allow plenty of space for recreational activities.

The Junior Republic is a school for boys who have run into trouble with the law. It has been a part of Litchfield for many years. Kevin Holmgren came to the Junior Republic when he was 13 years old. A year later he was just about ready to leave and go to trade school. Kevin explained why the school was so important to him. "Other places . . . they just took you as a bad person, you know? Here at least, they give you a reason. They look at why you're having these problems and what they can do to help you with them and straighten you out."

The reasons for many of these problems are complicated. Poverty contributes to these problems. So do broken homes and the pressures of modern life. The Connecticut Junior Republic may not be the solution to far-reaching problems. But it is a place where one town tries to help some of the kids who have become victims and who otherwise might make the problems worse. It's a place that has given Kevin Holmgren a new lease on life.

Today, the Connecticut Junior Republic continues its work. It has set up a group home in East Hartford and organized other outreach programs. The approach sounds simple: deal with the sources of trouble, build self-esteem, and give a sense of direction. For more than eight hundred boys every year, the approach seems to be working.

Connecticut's Harbor Lights Still Shine

The East Coast of the United States has a rich history connected to the Atlantic Ocean. Connecticut is no exception. Although major changes have taken place in the fishing industry, you can still see evidence of its impact on Connecticut in Stonington and Mystic Seaport.

The history of the Portuguese fishing community in Stonington began in the 1840s in the Azores, which are islands that belong to Portugal. At that time the whaling industry was important in the Azores. But many young men joined whaling ships headed for America. Their real purpose for joining the whalers was to get a free ride to the New World—the land of opportunity.

Stonington was a popular whaling port at that time. That's where many of the young Portuguese sailors settled. Most tried to make their living by fishing. They were used to life on the ocean. The business of fishing is done year-round. It is extremely difficult work because the weather and the ocean can be harsh and dangerous.

Today the well-known Portuguese fishing community of Stonington has shrunk. Not many people make their living by fishing the old way any more. But many of the traditional celebrations still take place. One of these is the annual Blessing of the Fleet. This tradition now honors the members of the fishing community who were lost at sea. The event is usually held the last week of July. The first part of the celebration is a lobster festival. The next day a mass is said at St. Mary's Church, followed by a parade to the harbor. Crowds gather to watch as the

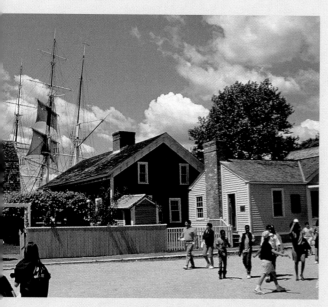

Many people view Mystic Seaport as a "living" museum.

ceremony of blessing the decorated fishing boats takes place. Then the entire fishing fleet leaves the harbor, just as it used to.

Mystic Seaport also pays its respects to Connecticut's whaling and fishing heritage. Docked in the harbor today are two very old ships. One is the *Australia*, the oldest active American sailing ship. The other ship is the *Charles W. Morgan*, the last of the wooden whaling ships. These two ships are more than just relics of the

past. Young people who are interested in learning sailing skills are invited to learn aboard these originals.

Many things have changed in Stonington and Mystic Seaport since the days of whale hunting and fishing. But one thing is not likely to change. That is the respect the residents have for those who braved the sea.

The pageantry of the Blessing of the Fleet goes back to the Portuguese tradition of blessing the fishing fleets.

Stonington still has people who make their living by fishing, but modern boats and equipment have replaced the wooden sailing ships of the past.

Looking Forward

In the years to come, Connecticut will have to face several challenges. Meeting those challenges will make new demands on the state's old traditional Yankee ingenuity.

In the early 1990s, unemployment became a major problem in Connecticut. The state's businesses searched for new products to replace the old ones. Much of the state's future will be in its growing high-tech industries. In the meantime, legalized gambling has brought in added income needed to support state programs.

As strange as this may sound, Connecticut's second problem has been caused by its beauty. People that move from one state to another usually do so because of jobs. Connecticut's population has remained steady because many people who live in the state don't work there. Instead they work in neighboring states like New York. They would rather live among the lush and rustic confines of Connecticut than move elsewhere.

The state's capital, Hartford, is a major industrial and commercial center. It also has a number of historical and cultural features.

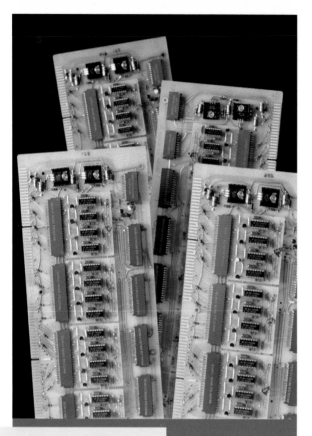

Connecticut's electronic parts industry is expected to continue growing at a steady pace throughout the 1990s.

The problem is that more and more people means less and less open land. The strains on the environment—especially the water and the air—have been great. In order to be sure that there will still be some open lands, the state set up a farmland preservation program in 1978. Rivers are being reclaimed for boating and swimming, and eventually they will be able to be used for drinking water. But not quite yet.

The third challenge lies in continuing to adapt to the demands of today's marketplace. In the past, Connecticut manufacturing has shown that it can be flexible, changing with the times. There is every reason to believe that flexibility will continue in the future. Already, Connecticut is one of the two or three leaders in the country in new high-tech industries.

The future in Connecticut may not be easy. But then it wasn't easy for a small state with almost no farmland and few natural resources to survive and prosper back in 1776. And Connecticut did it. It wasn't easy for this Yankee stronghold to accept thousands of immigrants from other countries and workers from other states. And Connecticut has been doing it.

Difficult tasks seem to bring out the best in Connecticut. In fact, if it were easy, it probably wouldn't be Connecticut.

Important Historical Events

1614 Adriaen Block sails up the Connecticut River. He explores the area and claims it for the Dutch.

1633 The Dutch act on their claim to the region by building the House of Hope at Hartford. Settlers from Plymouth, led by William Holmes, establish the first English settlement, a post at Windsor.

1636 The English settlements of Hartford, Wethersfield, and Windsor unite to form the Connecticut Colony.

1637 The Pequots are defeated by the colonists in the Pequot War.

1638 A group of wealthy Puritans, including Theophilus Eaton and Reverend John Davenport, establishes a settlement at Quinnipiac, now called New Haven.

1639 The Connecticut Colony adopts the Fundamental Orders of Connecticut.

1662 King Charles II of England gives a land charter to John Winthrop, Jr., of the Connecticut Colony, which combines the New Haven Colony and the Connecticut Colony.

1665 New Haven and Connecticut colonies are formally united.

1675 Sir Edmund Andros, governor of several other New England colonies, tries to gain control of Connecticut.

1687 Andros comes to Hartford and demands Connecticut's charter.

1701 Yale University is founded in New Haven, and the town is made the colonial capital jointly with Hartford.

1774 The first law school in the United States is founded at Litchfield.

1776 On June 14 Connecticut passes a resolution favoring independence from Great Britain.

1788 Connecticut becomes the fifth state to join the Union when it approves the U.S. Constitution on January 9. Hartford becomes the site of the first wood mill in New England.

1797 Eli Whitney, using a new assembly-line technique, opens a firearms factory in Whitneyville, near New Haven.

1808 Eli Terry is the first to make clocks with the mass-production techniques.

1810 The nation's first silk mill is established in Mansfield.

1844 The New York and New Haven railroads are chartered.

1881 The University of Connecticut is founded at Storrs.

1910 The U.S. Coast Guard Academy opens in New London.

1954 The world's first nuclear-powered submarine is built and launched at Groton.

1965 Connecticut adopts a new state constitution. Its legislative districts are redrawn to provide representation based on population.

1974 Ella Grasso becomes the first woman in any state elected in her own right to the office of governor.

1979 Connecticut passes a law forbidding the construction of more nuclear power plants in the state.

1991 Connecticut establishes a state income tax.

The flag presents a shield with three grapevines on a blue background. The grapevines symbolize the transplanted European settlers in the new land. The translation of the Latin motto below the shield is "He Who Is Transplanted Still Sustains."

Connecticut Almanac

Nickname. The Constitution State

Capital. Hartford

State Bird. Robin

State Flower. Mountain laurel

State Tree. White oak

State Motto. *Quit Transtulit Sustinet* (He Who Is Transplanted Still Sustains)

State Song. "Yankee Doodle"

State Abbreviations. Conn. (traditional); CT (postal)

Statehood. January 9, 1788, the 5th state

Government. Congress: U.S. senators, 2; U.S. representatives, 6. State Legislature: senators, 36; representatives, 151. 169 towns (no county governments)

Area. 5,006 sq mi (12,966 sq km), 48th in size among the states

Distances. north/south, 73 mi (117 km); east/west, 100 mi (161 km)

Elevation. Highest: Mount Frissell, 2,380 ft (725 m). Lowest: sea level, along Long Island Sound. Coastline: 618 mi (995 km)

Population. 1990 Census: 3,295,669 (6% increase over 1980), 27th among the states. Density: 658 persons per sq mi (254 per sq km). Distribution: 79% urban, 21% rural. 1980 Census: 3,107,576

Economy. *Agriculture:* greenhouse and nursery products, eggs, milk, tobacco. *Fishing:* shellfish (clams, lobsters, scallops) *Manufacturing:* transportation equipment, machinery, fabricated metal products, scientific instruments, chemicals, electrical equipment, printed materials. *Mining:* crushed stone

State Flower: Mountain laurel

State Bird: Robin

State Seal

Annual Events

★ Civil War Battles and Encampment in Hammonasset State Park (April)

★ Daffodil Festival in Meriden (April)

★ Dogwood Festival in Fairfield (May)

★ Bluegrass Festival in Preston (June)

★ Blessing of the Fleet in Stonington (June or July)

★ Round Hill Scottish Games in Stamford (July 4)

★ Taste of History in Mystic Seaport (August)

★ Hot Air Balloon Festival in Plainville (August)

★ Huckleberry Finn Raft Race in New Preston (September)

Places to Visit

★ Stamford Museum and Nature Center in Stamford

★ Maritime Center in South Norwalk

★ Mark Twain's mansion in Hartford

★ Mystic Seaport in Mystic

★ Colonial buildings throughout Connecticut

★ Connecticut River Museum in Essex

★ Gillette Castle in Hadlyme

★ National Theatre of the Deaf in Chester

★ Nathan Hale Schoolhouses in East Haddam and New London

Index

African Americans, 19, 34
agriculture, 14, 28–29
Alcott, Amos Bronson, 34
Algonquins, 9
Andros, Sir Edmund, 12
art, 36
Block, Adriaen, 9, 10
Bushnell, David, 16
Charter Oak, 12
Civil War, 16
Coleco, 26
colonization, 10–12
Congregational Church, 11
Connecticut Colony, 10, 11
Connecticut Compromise, 14
Connecticut Junior Republic, 38–39
Connecticut Leather Company, 26
Connecticut River, 9
Constitutional Convention, 13
Crandall, Prudence, 34
Declaration of Independence, 13
East Hartford, 39
education, 34, 38–39
Edwards, Jonathan, 34
England, 10, 11, 13, 20, 21–23
environment, 44
Eugene O'Neill National Playwrights' Conference, 37
Eugene O'Neill Theater Center, 37
fishing, 37, 40–41
Fundamental Orders, 11, 14
Gallaudet, Thomas H., 34
gambling, 19, 43
Gillette, William, 35, 36
Gillette Castle, 36
Goodspeed Opera House, 37
Goodyear, Charles, 16, 17
government, state and local, 18
Groton, 18
Hanks, Horatio, 16
Hanks, Rodney, 16
Hartford, 9, 10, 12, 19, 28, 35, 43
Hartford Courant, The, 33
Holmes, Sherlock, 35

Hooker, Thomas, 10, 11
House of Hope, 10
immigration, 14, 16
insurance, 28
inventions, 15–16, 30
Kaman, Charles H., 30–31
Kaman Corporation, 30–31
    Hamer guitar, 31
    K-MAX helicopter, 31
    Ovation guitar, 31
Lincoln, Abraham, 34
Litchfield, 38, 39
literature, 34–36
manufacturing, 6, 13, 15–16, 17, 25–28, 44
Massachusetts Bay Colony, 10
mass production, 15–16, 17, 25
Merriam, Charles, 22–23
Merriam, George, 22–23
Merriam-Webster company, 23
Mohegan, 9, 10
Mystic Harbor, 34
Mystic Seaport, 6, 34, 40–41
    Australia, the, 41
    Charles W. Morgan, the, 41
Narragansett, 10
National Critics Conference, 37
National Institute for Theater, 37
National Theatre of the Deaf, 37
Native Americans, 9, 10
Netherlands, 9, 10
New Britain, 37
New England Air Museum, 26
New Haven, 11, 12, 33, 36
New Haven Colony, 11
New York City, 25
O'Neill, Eugene, 36
O'Neill, James, 35–36
Pequot, 9, 10, 19
Picasso, Pablo, 36
population, 14, 16, 43
Portugal, 40
Prout, Mrs., 16
religious freedom, 11
Revolutionary War, 13

riots, 19
St. Mary's Church, 40
Sherman, Roger, 14, 15
slavery, 10, 34
Stonington, 37, 40–41
Stowe, Harriet Beecher, 34
Streep, Meryl, 37
technology, 16, 27–28
Terry, Eli, 16
Thames River, 9
theater, 35, 37
tourism, 6, 29
Turtle, the, 13
Twain, Mark, 34–35
unemployment, 26, 43
U.S. Constitution, 6, 11, 14
U.S. Naval Submarine Base, 18
    Nautilus, the, 17, 18
U.S. Patent Office, 15
Wadsworth Atheneum, 36
war materials, 13, 15, 16, 17
Washington, George, 13
Waterford, 37
Webster, Noah, 20–23, 34
    American Dictionary of the English Language, An, 22
    American Spelling Book, The, 20
    Blue-Backed Speller, 20
    Compendious Dictionary of the English Language, 20
Weicker, Lowell, Jr., 19
West Hartford, 20, 34
Wethersfield, 10
whaling, 34, 40–41
Whitney, Eli, 15, 16, 33
Wilson, Sloan, 35
Windsor, 10, 11
Windsor Locks, 26
World War I, 17
World War II, 17
Yale University, 20, 33, 36
    Yale Repertory Theatre, 37
    Yale School of Drama, 37